AF469744

A MATHEMATICAL
WOULD YOU RATHER
≫ GAME BOOK ≪

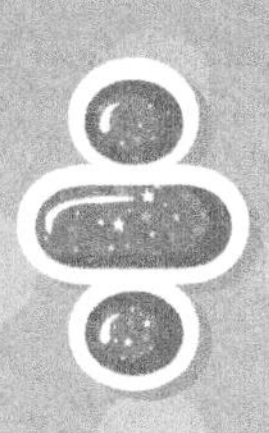

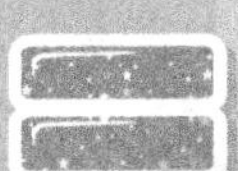

MATHSTICKS

Looking for an interactive way to keep maths alive and engage the whole family?

...then this is for you.

"A Mathematical Would You Rather..." is a fun, problem solving game where you and other players have to choose between two mathematical situations.

Once you've settled on a choice you can explore why you made that particular choice and then go on to prove it!

It's an amazing way to bringing maths issues into 'real life' in a quirky and interesting way. Also, simply asking a player to explain their reasons for a choice boosts their understanding, offers a great way to share strategies and ensures everyone understands and practices mathematical skills.

Ideal for ages 8-104 years. Yes, adults will enjoy talking through the challenges just as much as children!

How to Use This Book

If you are playing with another person, you each take it in turns to choose a question.

Every question begins with the words **"Would You Rather..."** and then there are two choices.

- Read the question together.

- Then, both of you should make your own choice.

- Next, talk to each other.

- How did you decide on **your** choice?

- Do you agree, or have you made different choices? It doesn't matter who is right or wrong - the fun is in sharing ideas.

- What calculations did you do?

- Can one of you convince the other that their answer is the best?

All of the questions can be answered by using mathematical skills and knowledge.

If you are playing alone, choose a question.

- Think about the choices, which one seems best to you?

- How do you know?

- What calculations did you do?

- How would you convince someone else that that is the best choice?

- Was it a tricky question or an easy one?

- Can you find another question that is similar?

- Can you make up your own **Mathematical Would You Rather** questions?

All of the questions can be answered by using mathematical skills and knowledge.

FROM

MATHSTICKS.COM

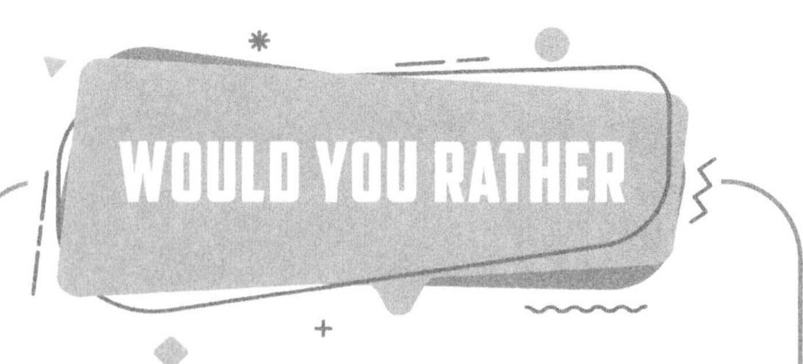

Read from quarter-to-ten in the morning until 12:20,

OR

read for 2 hours?

[You **love** reading]

Have the sum of the
first six odd numbers

OR

the sum of the first
five even numbers?

[you like big numbers]

Sort through one 5kg
pile of recycling

OR

six 700g piles of recycling?

Have a music player
that holds 10,000 three-
minute songs

OR

one that holds 600
hours of music?

Have half of five apples or

OR

a quarter of six apples?

[you **love** apples]

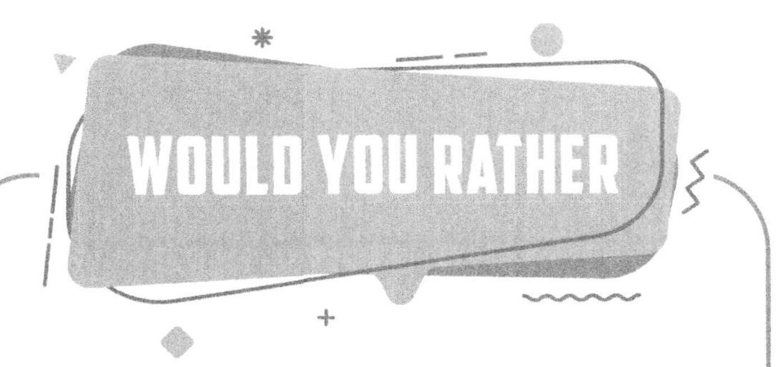

Play a fun game for
750 seconds

OR

a quarter of an hour?

Buy all seven of your favourite authors books for £3.99 each

OR

a huge volume of all the stories for £24.99

Have the number that is
halfway between
87 and 121

OR

double the number that
is halfway 50 and 90?

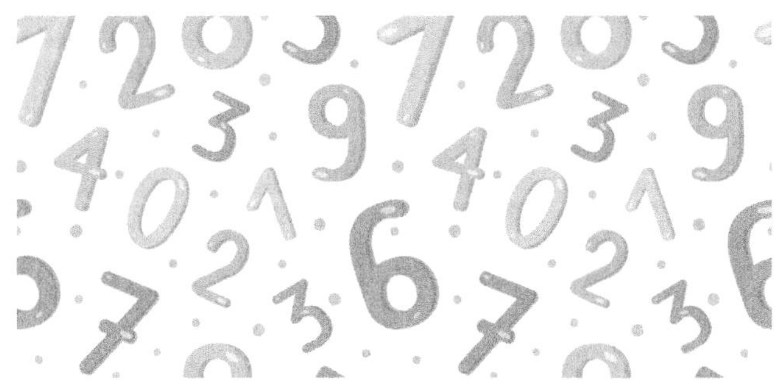

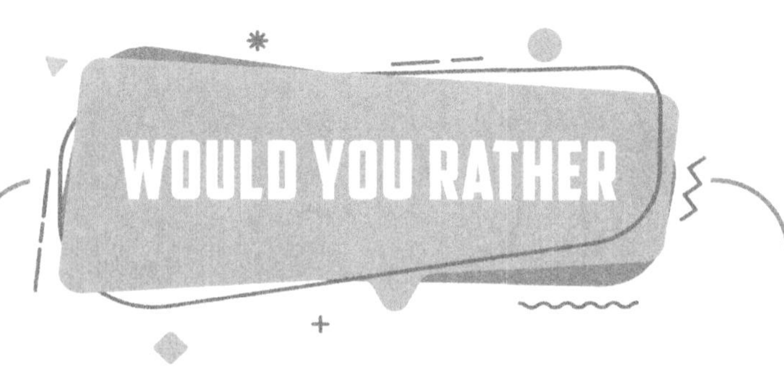

Go swimming on
26th March

OR

27th March?

[you only enjoy swimming on Fridays]

Sit in a traffic jam for
a third of an hour

OR

a fifth of 1 hour 50 minutes?

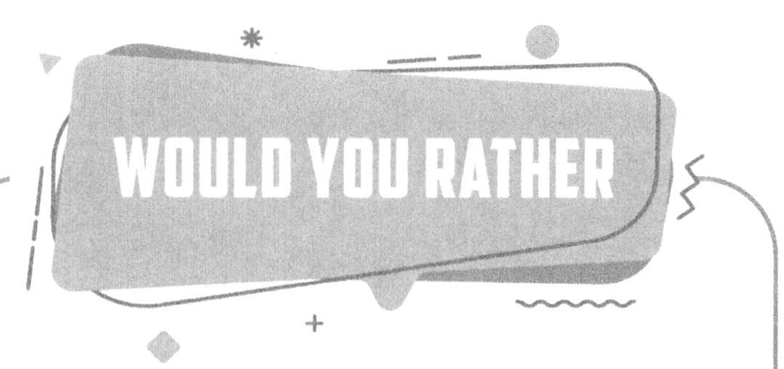

Buy a zoo pass that gives you a week's access for £49

OR

7 individual day tickets for £11 each?

The sum of all the
spots you can see

OR

the sum of all the
spots you can't see?

Be given 5/8 of a pizza

OR

a third of two pizzas?

[You **love** pizza]

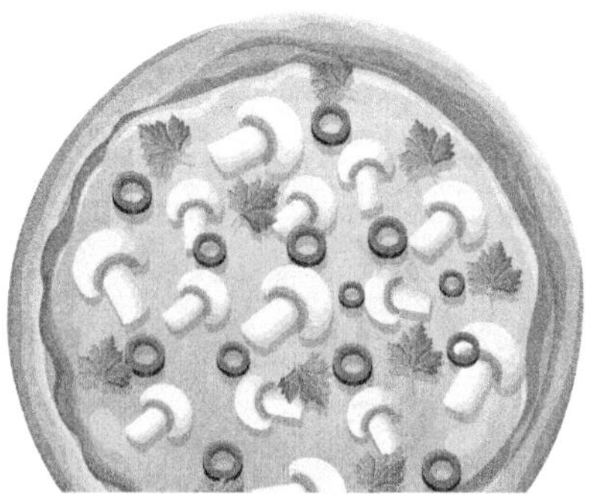

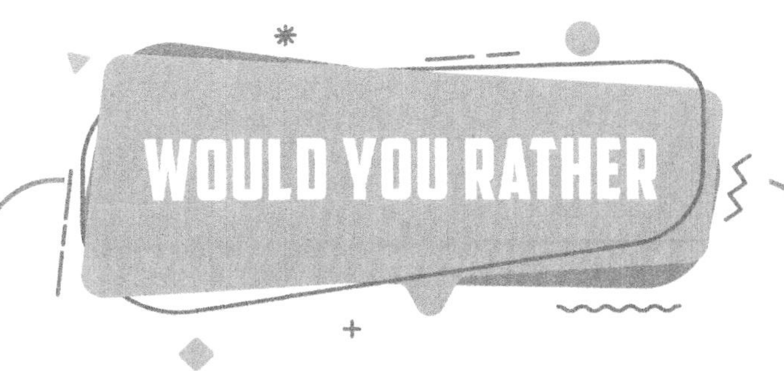

Own a magic crystal that
doubles in size every day

OR

one which triples in
size every other day?

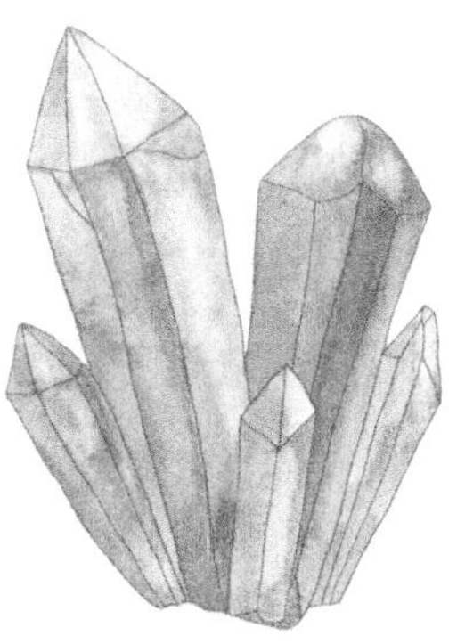

Buy chocolate bars
for 70p each

OR

a pack of six bars for £3.50

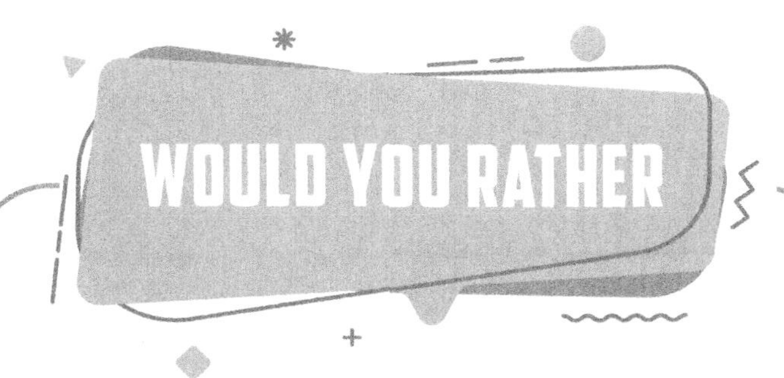

Be like Becky who scored 1360 points on her tablet game

OR

like Luke who scored 2855, but then lost 462 points?

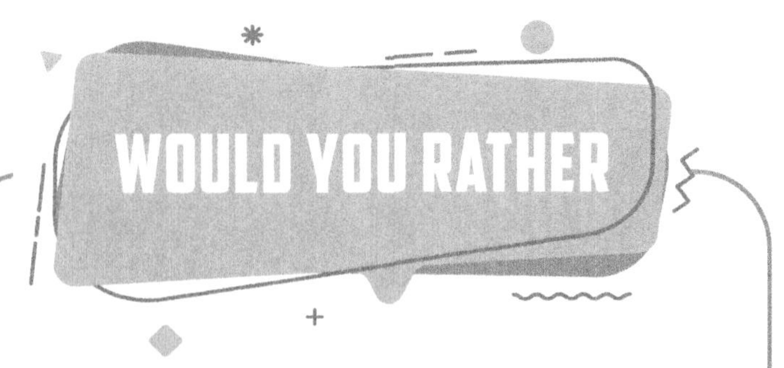

Have the sum of all
the grey numbers

OR

the sum of all the
white numbers?

9	8	8	9	10
20	14	20	16	20
20	7	10	7	20
5	12	13	4	18

Have the number

OR

the number

1	2	3
4	5	6
7	8	9

Say, "Always!"

OR

say, "Never!"?

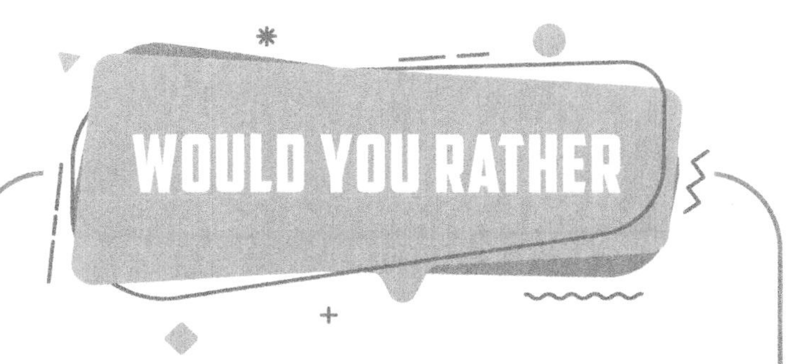

Have a third of LXVI

OR

three quarters of 140?

Go on holiday for 56 days

OR

for seven and a half weeks?

Run the length of the playing field four times

OR

run all around the perimeter once.

[The field is 24m wide, 48m long, and you love running]

Have the number of

OR

Wait a tenth of an hour

OR

400 seconds?

Buy 3 cupcakes at £1.75 each

OR

a pack of eight for £12.00?

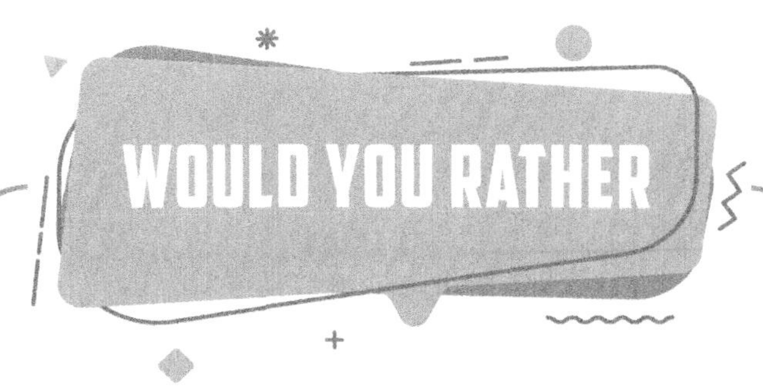

Have the sum of all
the numbers in 'A'

OR

the sum of all the
numbers in 'B'

[complete the sudoku]

	5				
4		6		1	
			2		
	1	2		4	6
				6	
3					

A →

B ←

Be half as old as Ian
who was born in 1982

OR

twice as old as Sally who
was born in 2009?

Accidentally pay £2.50
instead of £2.05

OR

lose 60p?

Have the number
of triangles

OR

the number of
quadrilaterals?

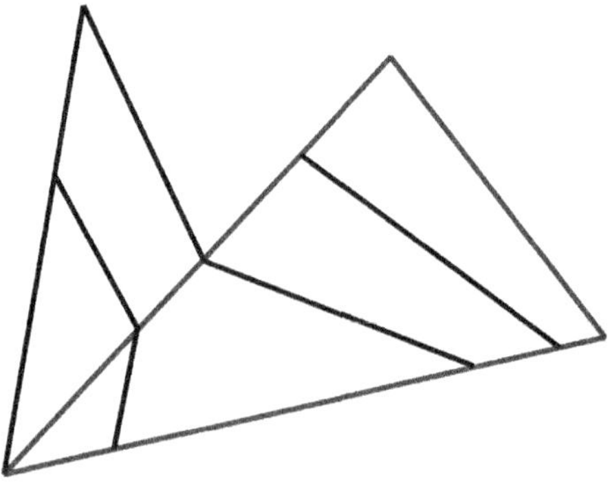

Have

🌙 × ☀ + ☺ × 🐟

OR

🐟 × 🌙 + ☺ × ☀

☀ ☀ 🌙
☀ ☀ ☀
+ 🐟 ☺ 🌙 ☀
____
1 2 1 2

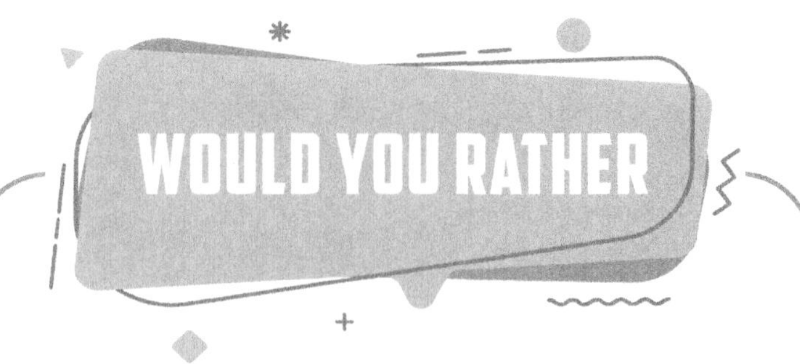

Have an S-23 phone charger

OR

an Sp-5 phone charger

The S23 achieves full charge in 250 minutes

The Sp-5 achieves full charge in three hours

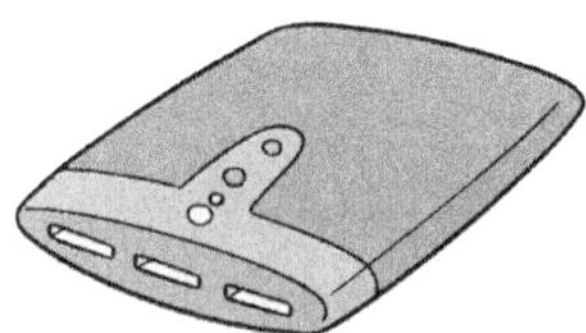

Have a pencil case that
is 300 millimetres long

OR

one that is 0.24m long?

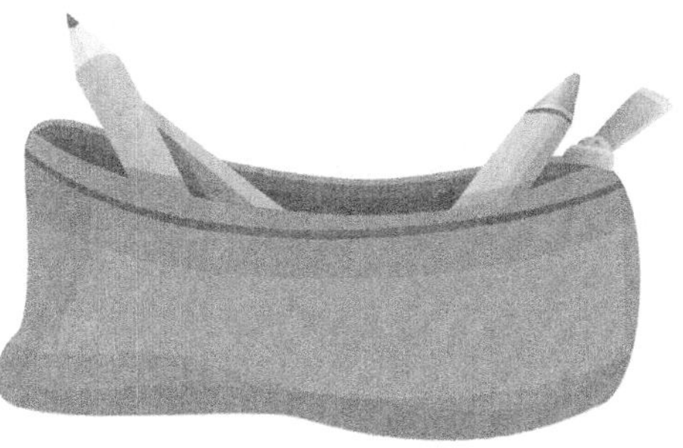

Have the sum of the five largest numbers in grey

OR

the sum of the four largest numbers in white?

3	2	5	5	5	1
6	2	9	3	6	6
2	5	5	2	7	7
4	6	6	7	9	6
2	7	5	9	2	7

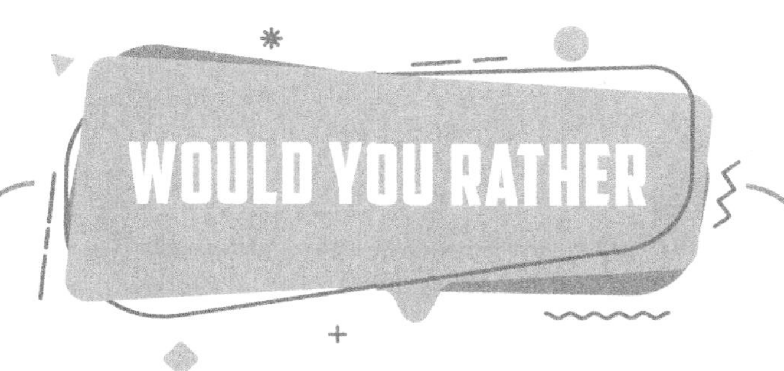

Have half the difference
between £153 and £37

OR

double the difference
between £120 and £84?

Pay £1.90 for a tub
of ice cream

OR

£9.00 for 5 tubs

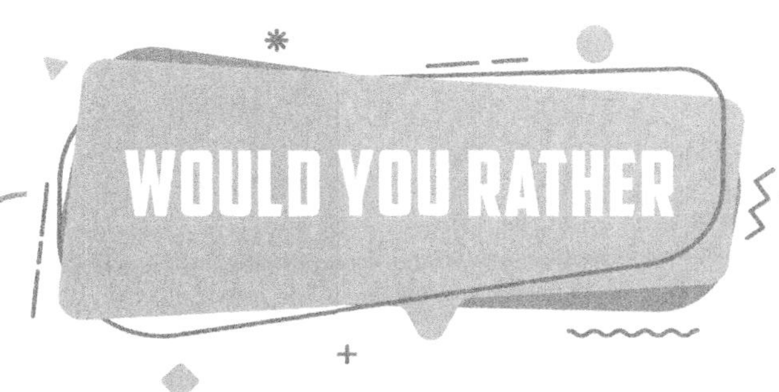

Have the value of the
word 'MAGICAL'

OR

the value of your
own first name?

Vowels are worth 40p,
consonants are
worth 5p.

Win a £5000 prize

OR

win £100 per week
for a year?

PRIZE
WINNER

Have the largest prime
number here

OR

double the smallest
square number?

[you like big numbers]

**1, 7, 13, 18, 25,
47, 49, 54, 69, 74**

Have a quarter of £32
plus half of £28

OR

three-quarters of £28
plus half of £32?

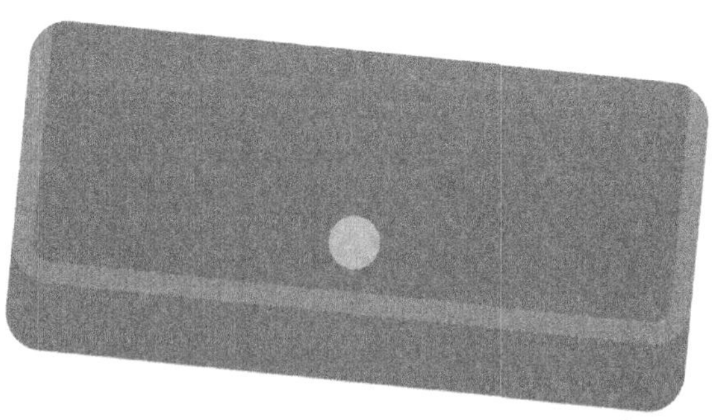

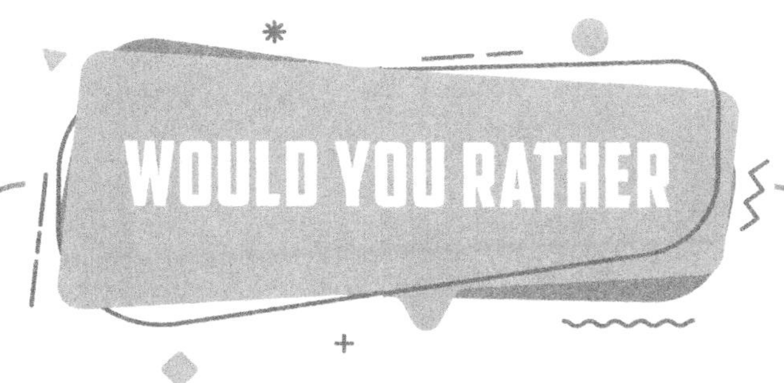

Have

🍌 × 🍓

OR

🍎 × 🍓

🍌 + 🍓 + 🍎 = 16

10 − 🍌 = 🍌

🍌 − 🍓 = 1

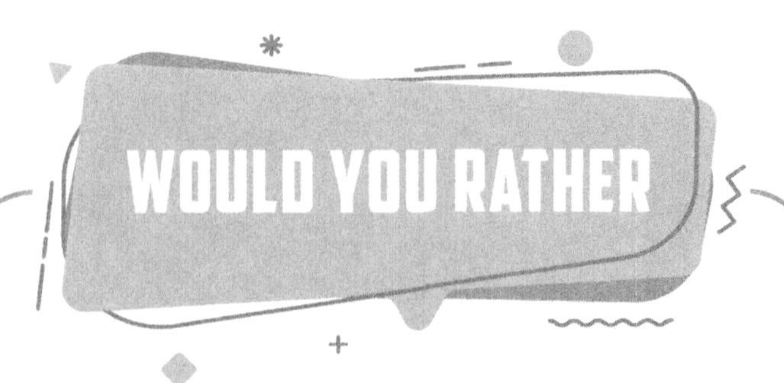

Be given a quarter of 140p plus half of 96p

OR

a half of 140p plus a quarter of 96p?

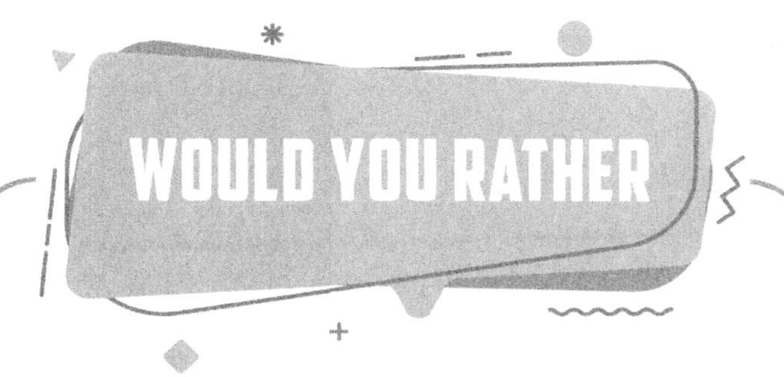

Have a square bedroom, with an area of 49m^2

OR

an oblong shaped bedroom, 6m by 8m?

[you are hoping to have the largest room]

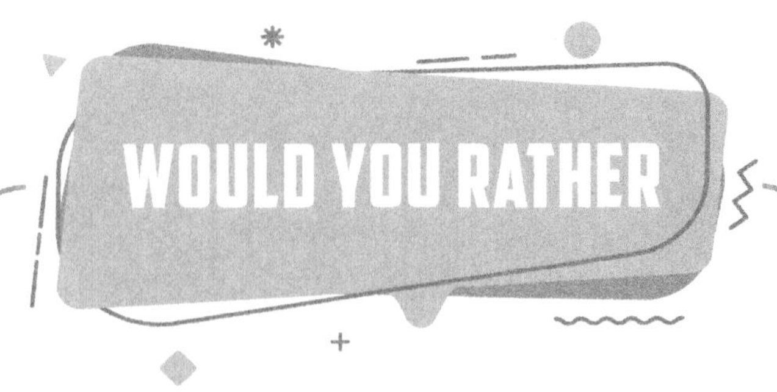

Have the number at 'A'

OR

the number at 'B'

[the number above is the sum
of the two numbers below]

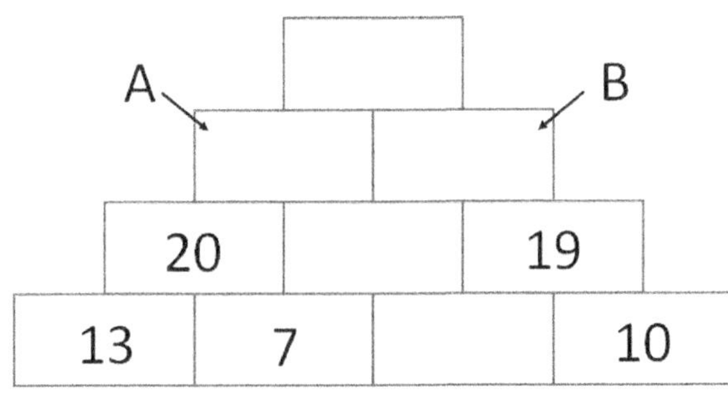

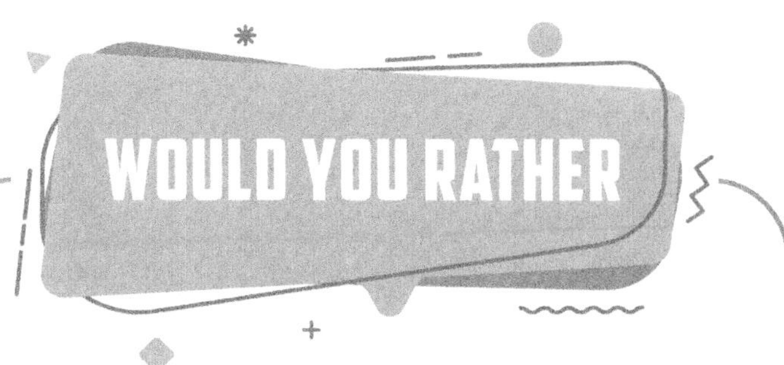

Have the seventh word
of the song '*Twinkle,
twinkle, little star,*'

OR

the twelth word of the song?

[you **like** long words]

Have four microwave
pies for £5.99

OR

seven microwave
pies for £9.95?

Be given half of £3.70

OR

a fifth of £9.00?

Have the sum of A and B

OR

the sum of B and C?

A	B	B	= 17
C	C	C	= 18
D	D	A	= 13

16 14 18

Be given £1 for every Tuesday in June and July

OR

£1 for every Wednesday in June and July?

Have the value of the river
T+H+A+M+E+S

OR

the value of the river
S+E+V+E+R+N

A	B	C	D	E	F	G	H	I	J	K	L	M
1	2	3	4	5	6	7	8	9	10	11	12	13

N	O	P	Q	R	S	T	U	V	W	X	Y	Z
14	15	16	17	18	19	20	21	22	23	24	25	26

Have the sum of the first four numbers that start with the letter 'f'

OR

the sum of the first three numbers that start with the letter 't'?

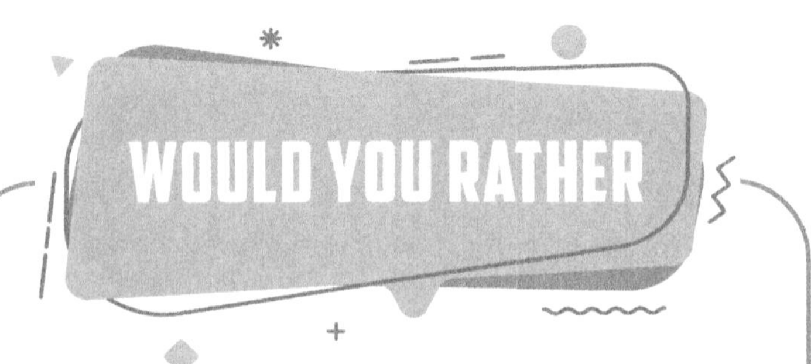

Double the difference
between 16 and 62

OR

50% of the difference
between 19 and 91?

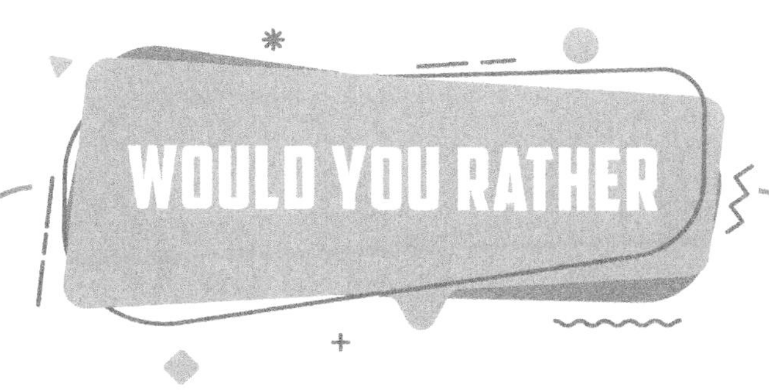

Say angle 'X' was 56°

OR

say angle 'X' was 54°?

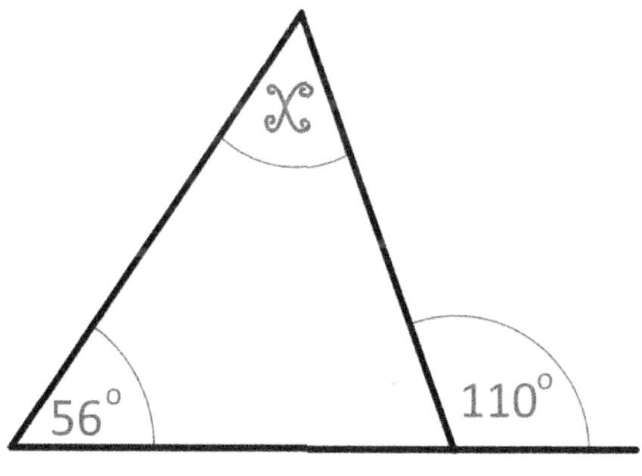

WOULD YOU RATHER

Share with your friend, a 4 by 6 block of chocolate,

OR

share a 3 by 8 block of chocolate?

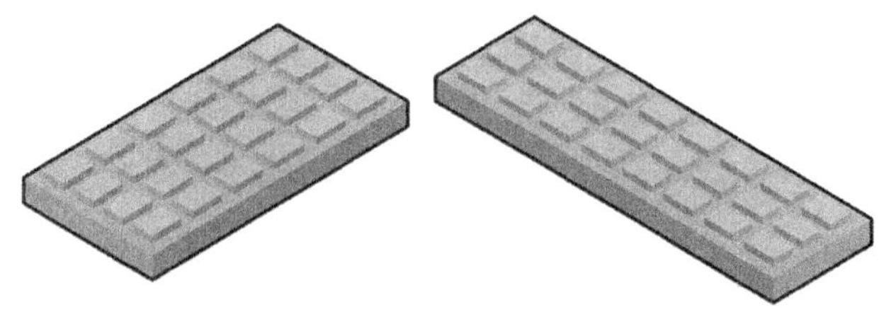

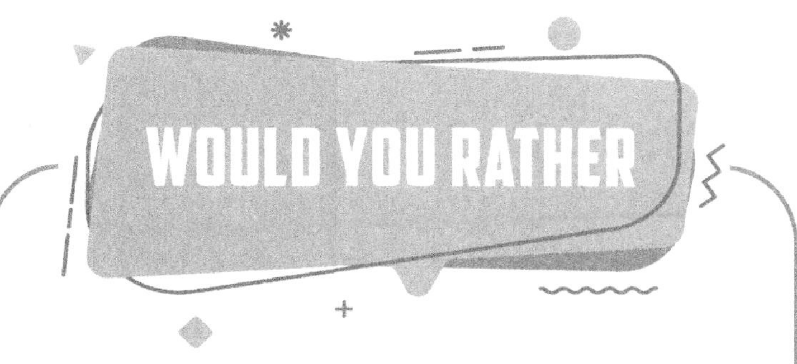

Have half of CXVI

OR

triple XXXVII?

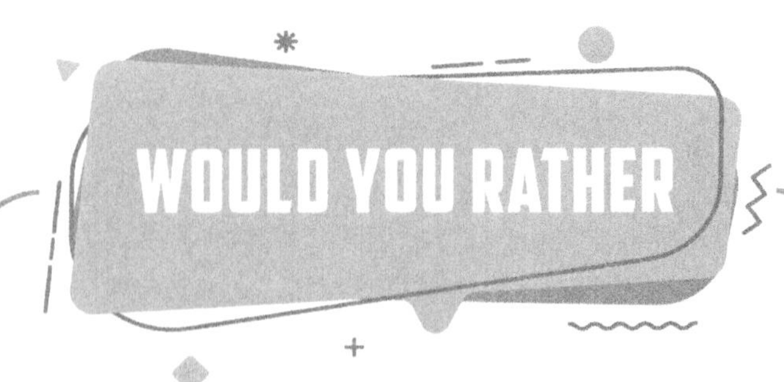

Have the value of the hundredths in the number below

OR

the value of the thousandths?

0.2573

Have 78 x 9

OR

7 x 89?

[you're hoping for the biggest number]

Have the white area

OR

the area shaded in grey?

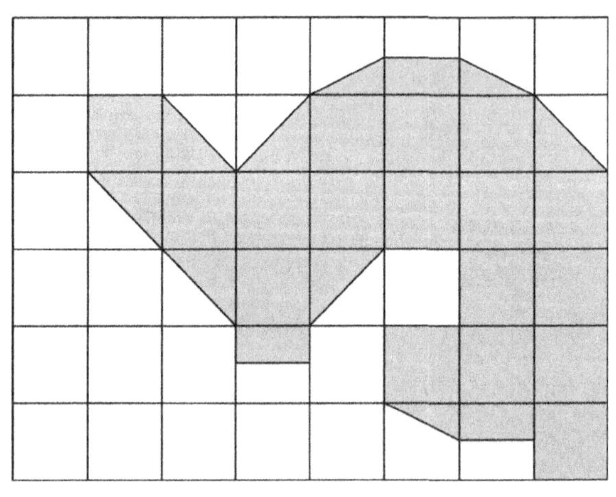

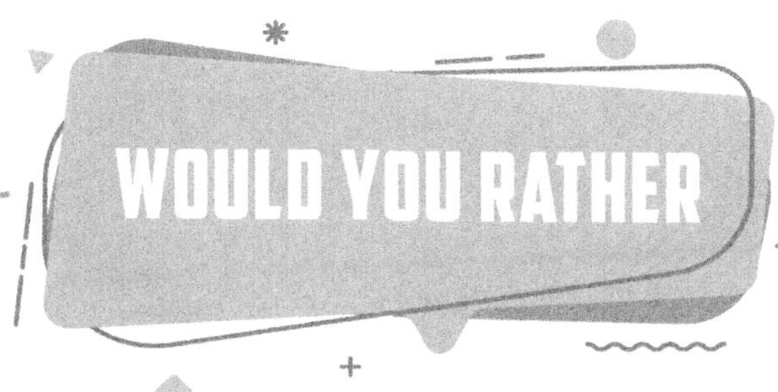

Have the number of

$$(\text{umbrella} - \text{foot}) \times \text{gift} + \text{star}$$

OR

$$(\text{foot} - \text{gift}) \times \text{star} + \text{umbrella}$$

Have five big bags with 12 biscuits in each one

OR

seven bags with nine biscuits in each bag?

Have the value of
M + U + L + T + I + P + L + Y

OR

the value of
D + I + V + I + S + I + O + N?

A=0.1, B=0.2, C=0.3,
and so on to Z=2.6

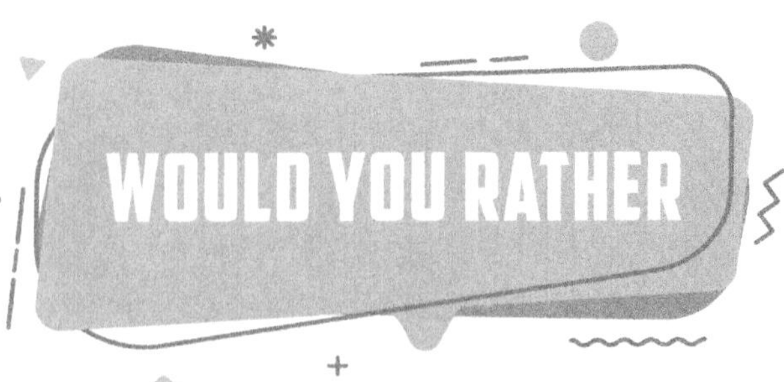

Have the
circumference

OR

four times the radius
of a circle?

[You **like** long distances]

WOULD YOU RATHER

Have the sum of the shaded numbers in 'A'

OR

the sum of the shaded numbers in 'B'?

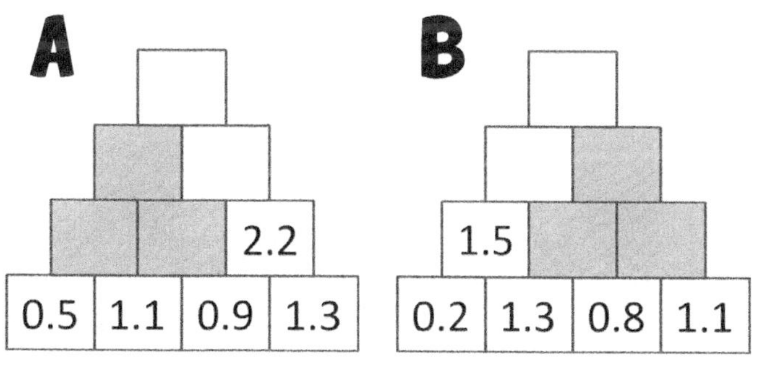

Have the number of faces
on a square pyramid

OR

the number of edges?

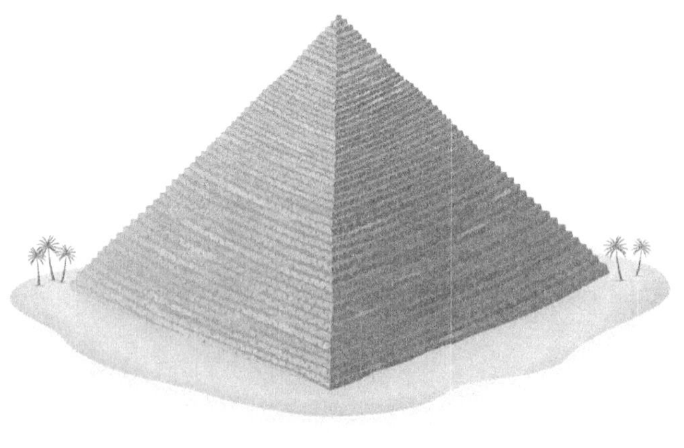

Have the difference
between 24 and 108

OR

half of 166?

[you **love** high numbers]

Have the product of the numbers on the right

OR

the product of the numbers on the left?

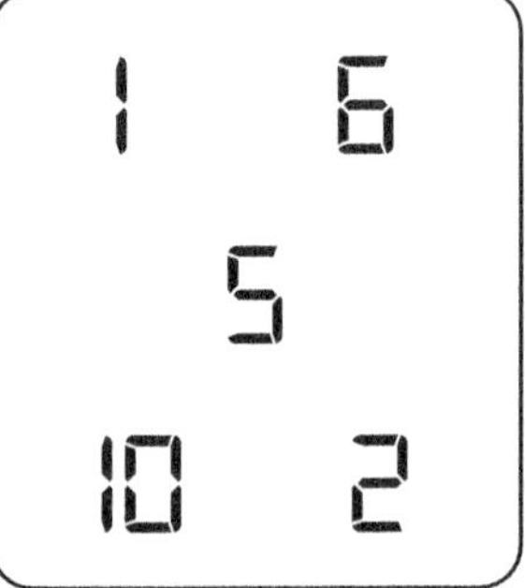

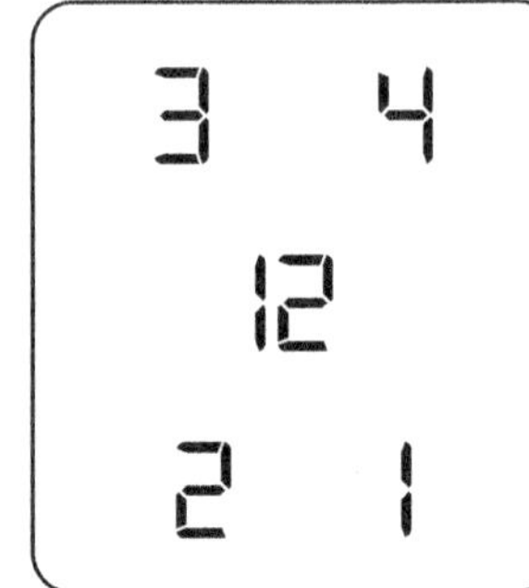

Buy a computer game, reduced by 20%

OR

the same game with £10 off?

Multiply

OR

Divide?

An airplane travels 3440 miles in one trip from London to New York.

How many miles would it travel in 5 trips to New York?

Have twenty-four

OR

sixty

[you are looking for the number
with the most factors]

Have the number

OR

the number

1	2	3
4	5	6
7	8	9

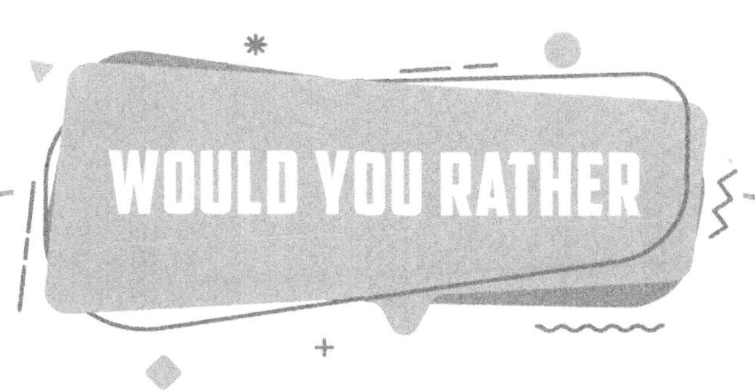

Grow a sunflower
like Jack

OR

grow one like
Jennifer?

Jack's sunflower grows
4cm every day.

Jennifer's sunflower
grows 1.5 inches
every day.

Have the mean of
10, 9, 8, 7 and 6

OR

the number of days
in a week?

Be given a box with 5
rows of 12 chocolates

OR

a box with 6 rows of
11 chocolates?

Have the sum of all
the grey numbers

OR

the sum of all the
white numbers?

(9) (13) (12) (9) (8)
(2) (1) (4) (1) (14)
(13) (7) (8) (8)
(2) (9) (11) (10) (13)
(13) (14) (6) (12) (12)

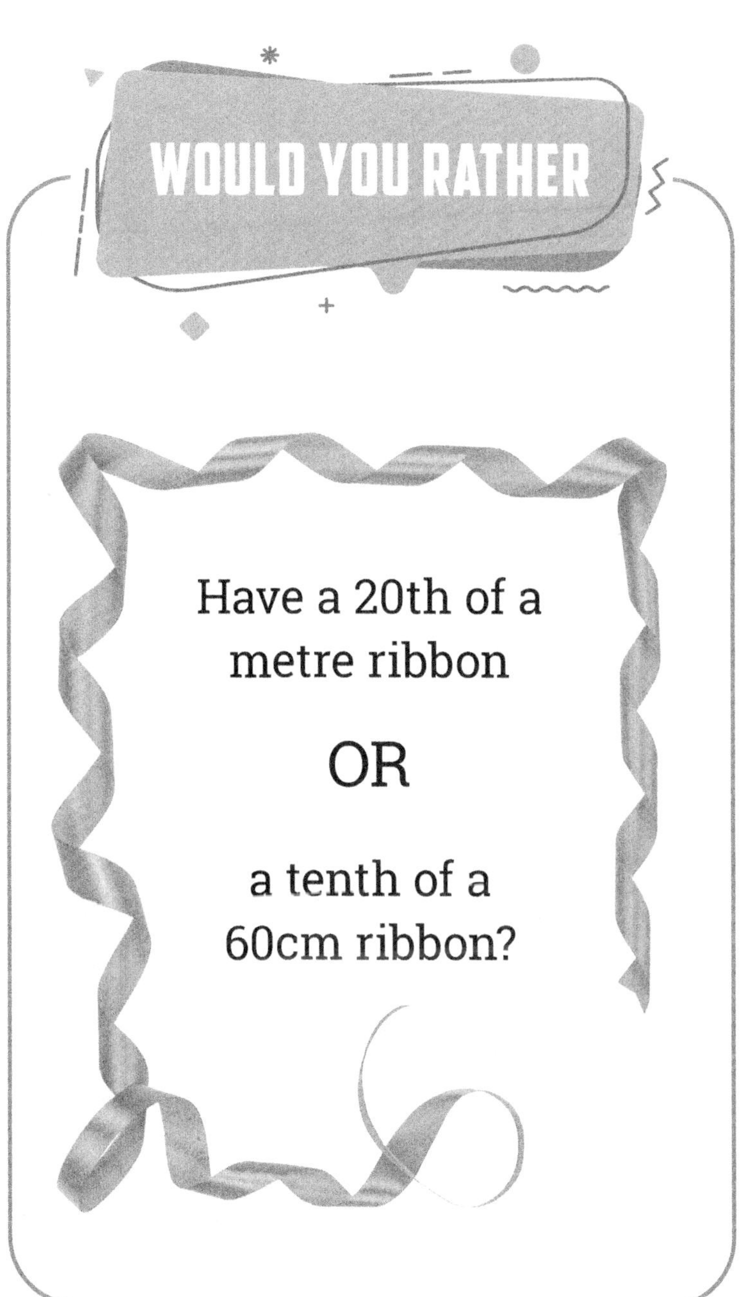
Have a 20th of a
metre ribbon

OR

a tenth of a
60cm ribbon?

Have LXX + XXVII

OR

CXI - XXIV

Be given 10% of £15

OR

75% of 180p?

Have the sum of the
numbers at 2,5 and 4,3

OR

the sum of the numbers
at 5,2 and 3,4?

5	0.18	0.19	0.22	0.73	0.34
4	0.52	0.78	0.34	0.91	0.84
3	0.45	0.81	0.44	0.36	0.66
2	0.73	0.34	0.63	0.02	0.53
1	0.09	0.98	0.61	0.74	0.79
	1	2	3	4	5

All the spots you can see

OR

all the spots you can't see?

Have the number at 'A'

OR

the number at 'B'

[the number above is the sum
of the two numbers below]

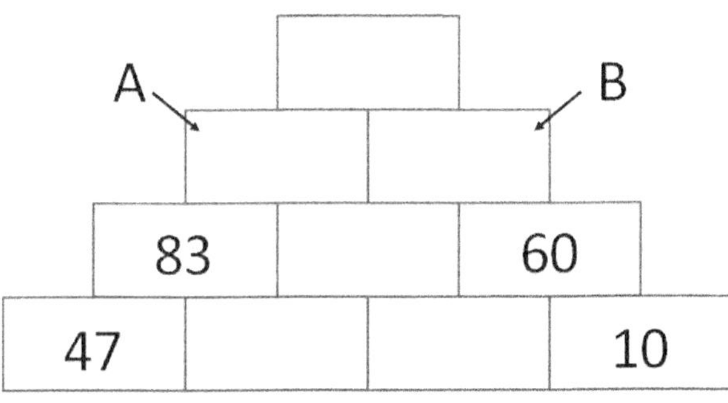

Have seven times **Q**

OR

twelve times **S**?

$$T + T = 6$$
$$Q + S + S = 10$$
$$Q + T = 7$$

Have the **mean** of all these numbers

OR

the **median**?

	13	3	9
1	6	11	2
14	7	2	12
	9	15	

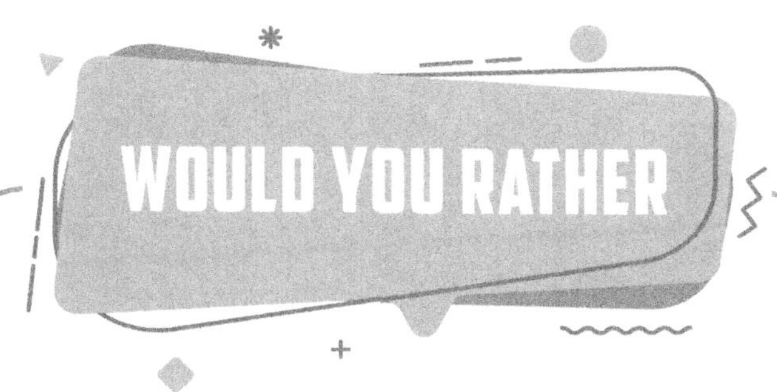

Have calculation '**A**'

OR

calculation '**B**'?

[You are hoping for the
smallest remainder]

A) $3062 \div 5$

B) $3283 \div 5$

Have half the product
of fifteen and twenty

OR

7/10 of 1000?

The number of the edges on both shapes

OR

double the number of faces on both shapes?

TRIANGULAR PRISM

CUBOID

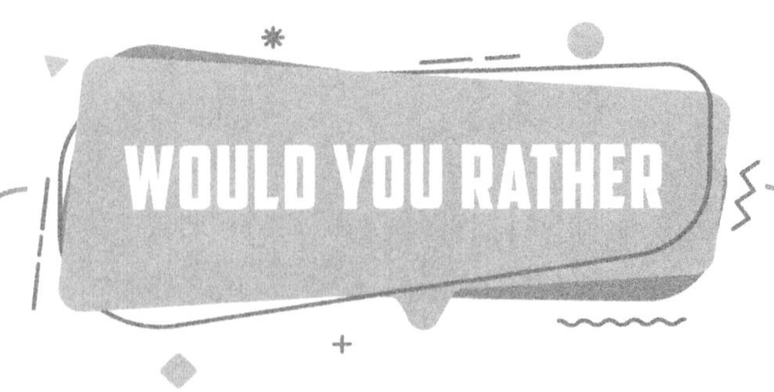

The value of
S+A+T+U+R+N

OR

the value of
J+U+P+I+T+E+R?

ABC DE	FGH IJ	KLM NOP	QRS TU	VWX YZ
1	2	3	4	5

Watch the Summer
Olympic games in 2030

OR

in 2032?

Have a stack of £1 coins
as wide as your hand

OR

a stack of £2 coins as
long as your thumb?

Have the sum of all four numbers in shape 'A'

OR

the sum of all four numbers in shape 'B'?

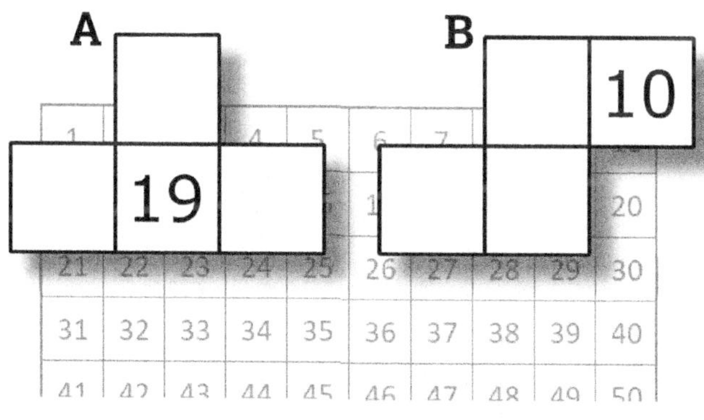

Be as old as Lance
(he's exactly 9 years old)

OR

be as old as Danielle
(she's 4000 days old)?

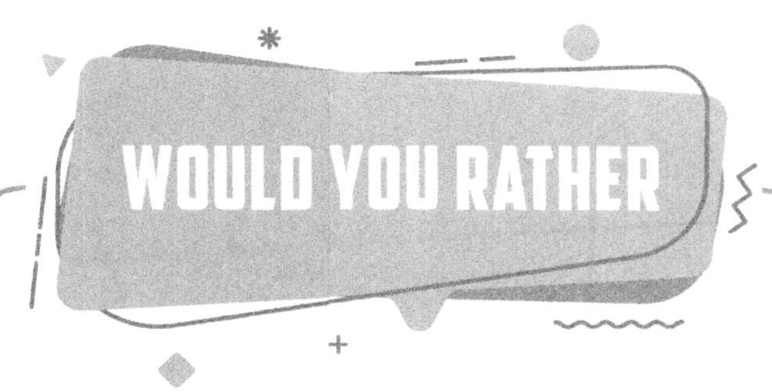

Have the number at 'A'

OR

the number at 'B'

[the number above is the sum of the two numbers below]

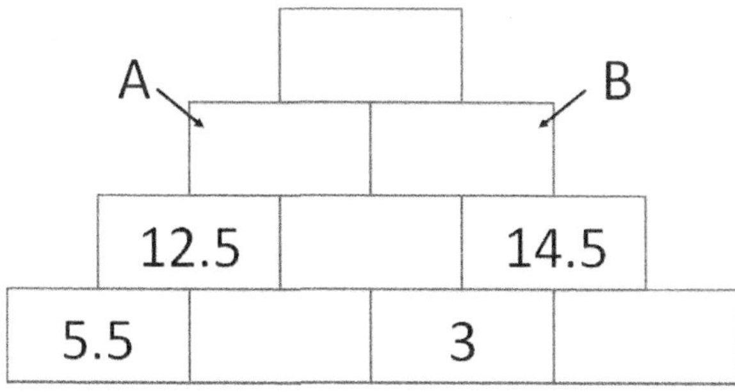

Walk 3 miles across
the hills on a cold
and wet afternoon

OR

walk 4 kilometres across
the same hills in the rain?

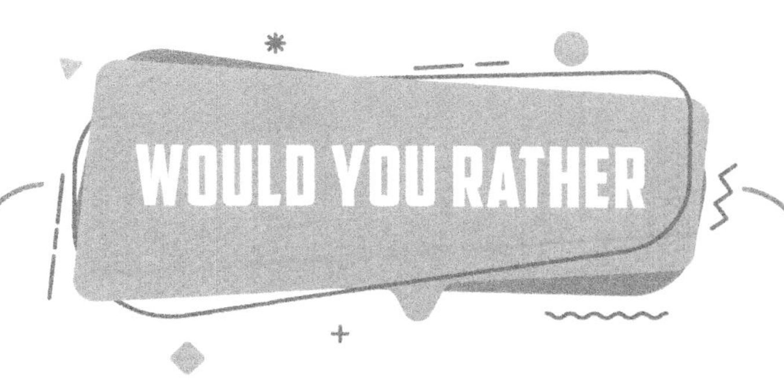

Have the total of all
the numbers in 'A'

OR

the total of all the
numbers in 'B'

[complete the sudoku]

A →
B →

1				2	
	6		5		
		3	1		
					5
				6	
		4			

Play a game for 150 minutes

OR

two and a quarter hours?

Have the number
of acute angles

OR

the number of right angles?

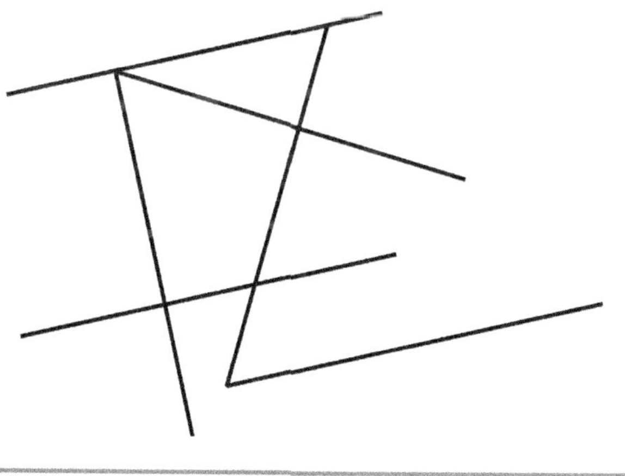

Go to the cinema
on July 20th

OR

July 26th?

[You must go on a Sunday]

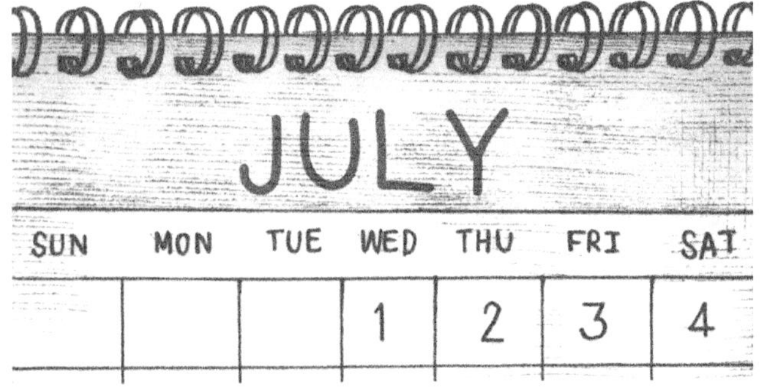

Have the number of

OR

Have a secret number that is half of 65 plus 19

OR

a secret number that is a quarter of 20 x 9?

Have the number of faces
on a dodecahedron

OR

the number of vertices
on a cube?

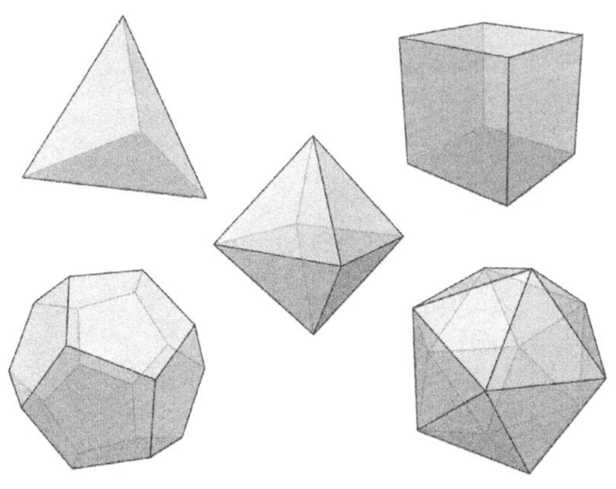

Have a third of the
difference between
£36 and £102

OR

one and a half times
the difference between
£88 and £104?

Have the sum of all the numbers on the right

OR

the sum of all the numbers on the left?

<table>
<tr><td>214</td><td>109</td></tr>
<tr><td colspan="2">211</td></tr>
<tr><td>116</td><td>117</td></tr>
</table>

<table>
<tr><td>137</td><td>95</td></tr>
<tr><td colspan="2">233</td></tr>
<tr><td>120</td><td>125</td></tr>
</table>

Say angle 'X' was 58°

OR

say angle 'X' was 68°?

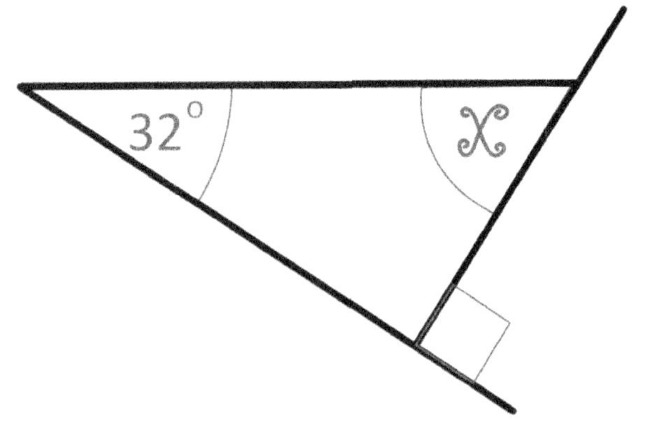

Have seven £1 coins
and three 20p coins

OR

seventeen lots of 50p?

Have A × B

OR

B × C?

A	**4**	B
10	**6**	**2**
3	**8**	C

This Magic Square uses the numbers 2 to 10 and has the same total horizontally, vertically and diagonally.

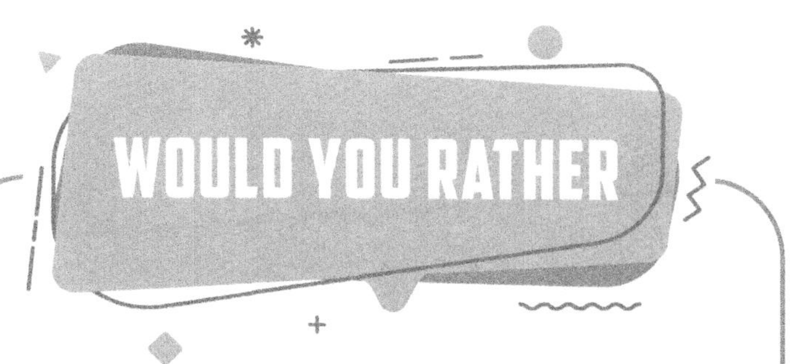

Have a carton with 0.6 litres of orange juice in it

OR

a half-full litre jug of juice?

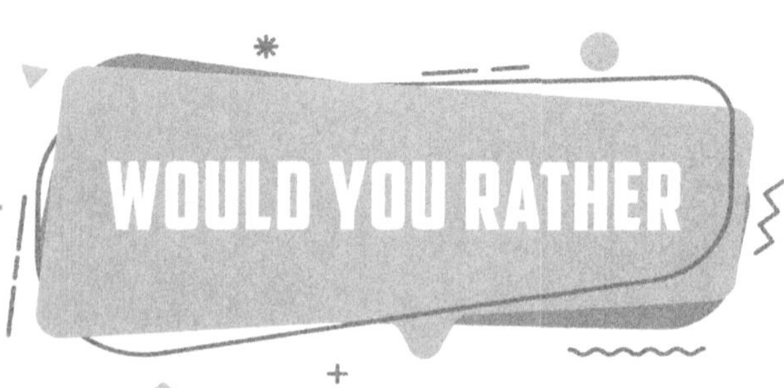

The value of
SI + LV + ER

OR

the value of
DR + AG + ON?

TO = 43

BE = 11

ABC DE	FGH IJ	KLM NOP	QRS TU	VWX YZ
1	2	3	4	5

Have the sum of the first
six prime numbers

OR

the sum of the first five
triangular numbers?

Have the number
of **this** page

OR

double the number of the
page with the picture
of the ice cream tub?

Have the difference
between 21.7 and 52.9

OR

double the difference
between 71.2 and 92.5?

WOULD YOU RATHER

Use 11 sticks to make a digital number

OR

12 sticks?

[You want to make the largest 2-digit multiple of five]

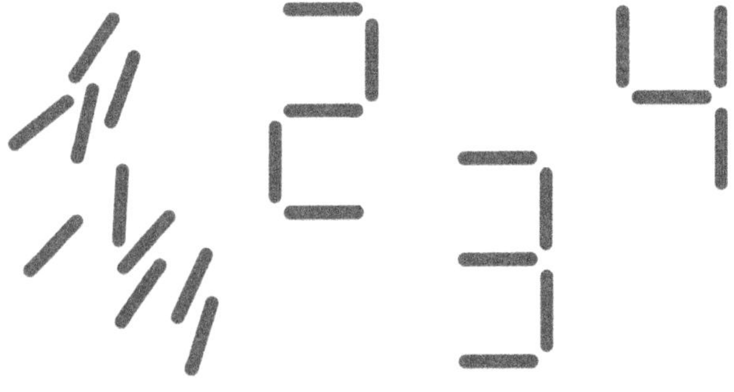

Have triple the difference
between 314 and 88

OR

40% of 850?

Have the amount at 'A'

OR

the amount at 'B'

[the number above is the sum
of the two numbers below]

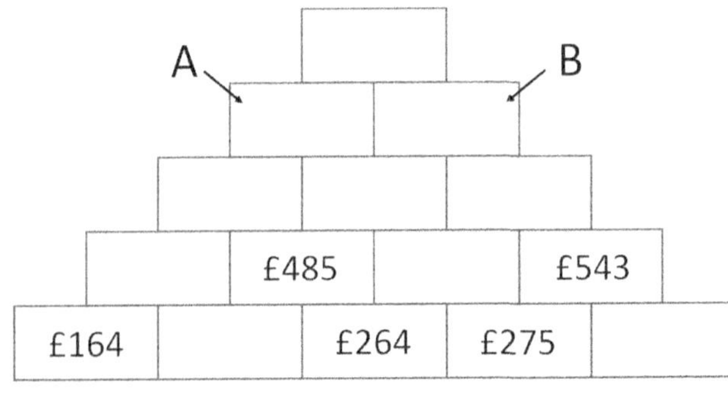

Have 7^2 reduced by 21

OR

half of 6^2.

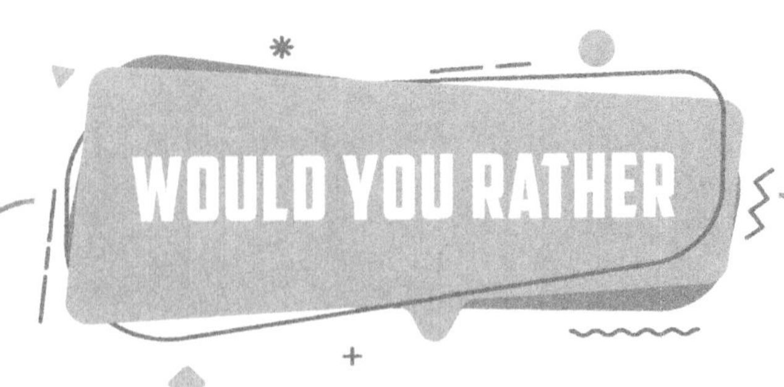

Have

 × 🍦

OR

 × 🏈

🍦 × 🏈 × 🐳 = 64

🏈 ÷ 🍦 = 🐳

🏈 × 🍦 = 16

Have a pocket filled with
one of every coin

(1p, 2p, 5p, 10p, 20p, 50p, £1, £2)

OR

seven 50p coins?

Share with a friend a box of chocolates with 7 rows of 8

OR

share a box with
6 rows of 9?

Have half the product
of five and eleven

OR

two-thirds of the
product of six and 12?

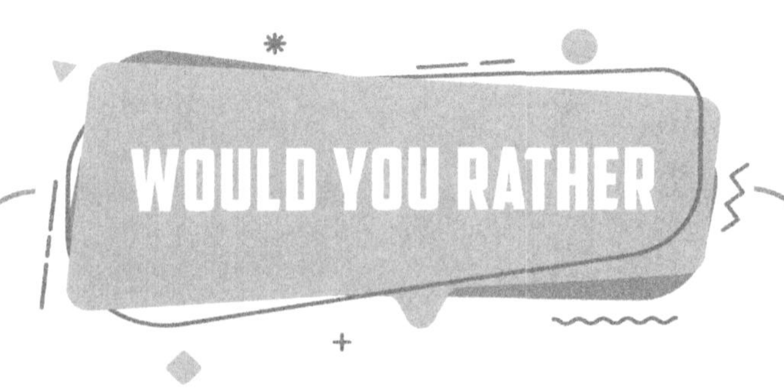

Have 4/5 of CL

OR

double LX?

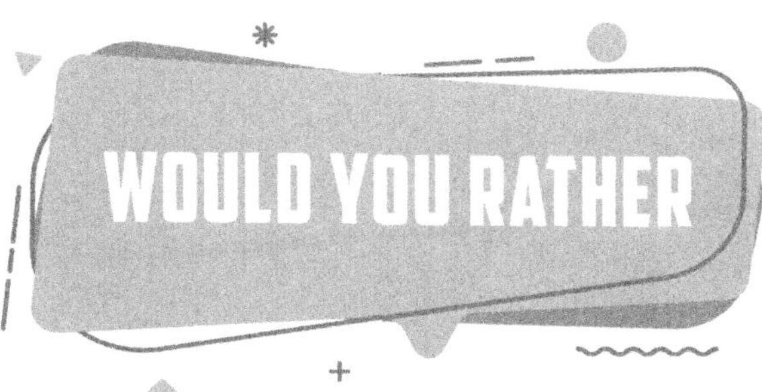

Multiply

OR

Divide?

Taylor is planning to stay in Paris. She rents a room in a hotel for £190 per night.

How much would she pay if she stayed in the hotel for 7 nights?

Dance from quarter-past-five in the afternoon until 18:40,

OR

dance for one-and-a-half hours?

[You **love** dancing]

Have the sum of the
numbers at
A,C + C,D + E,E

OR

the sum of the numbers at
C,A + D,C + A,A

	A	B	C	D	E
E	770	72	139	664	343
D	109	423	881	177	507
C	863	265	802	308	250
B	311	422	530	527	107
A	390	973	416	194	376

Have the number

OR

the number

$$\frac{1 \mid 2 \mid 3}{4 \mid 5 \mid 6}$$
$$\frac{}{7 \mid 8 \mid 9}$$

Have 4 x 5 x 6

OR

5 x 5 x 5?

[you're hoping for the biggest number]

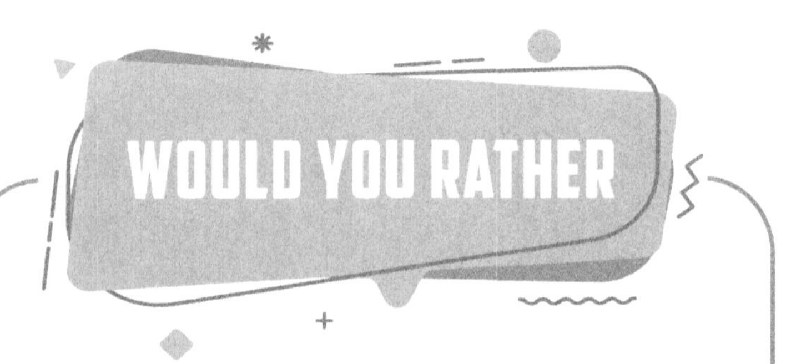

Have the sum of all
the numbers in '**A**'

OR

the sum of all the
numbers in '**B**'?

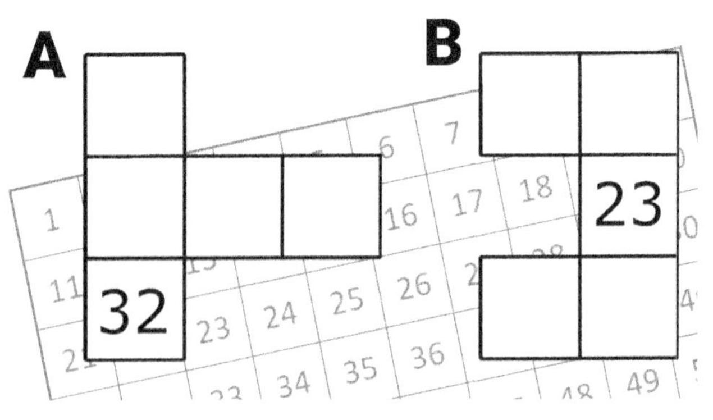

Have 12^2 plus 8^2

OR

half of 20^2.

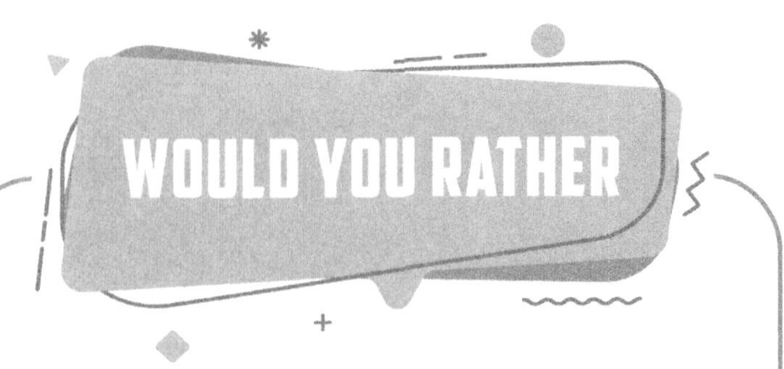

Have a quarter of
a third of 24

OR

a half of three-quarters
of a third of 24?

Be given two-thirds of £24.90

OR

a fifth of £75.50?

Have the number at 'A'

OR

the number at 'B'?

[the number above is the sum
of the two numbers below]

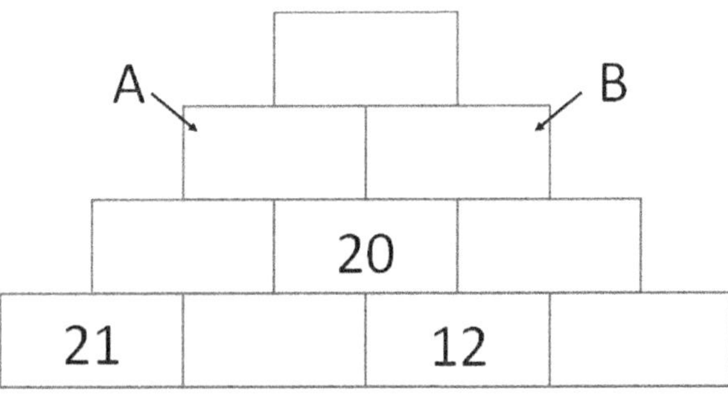

Have calculation '**A**'

OR

calculation '**B**'?

[You are hoping for the
smallest remainder]

A)   73962 ÷ 9

B)   65843 ÷ 9

The value of
(R+U)×(B+Y)

OR

the value of
(R×U)+(B×Y)?

ABC DE	FGH IJ	KLM NOP	QRS TU	VWX YZ
1	2	3	4	5

Have a stack of £1 coins
from the floor to your chin

OR

£200?

Have the sum of the two consecutive numbers which multiply to give 56

OR

the square root of 169?

75% of the difference
between 90 and 456

OR

Double the **mean**
of 155, 132, 121?

Have a kite

OR

a trapezium?

[You are trying to avoid parallel lines]

Have the amount at 'A'

OR

the amount at 'B'

[the number above is the sum
of the two numbers below]

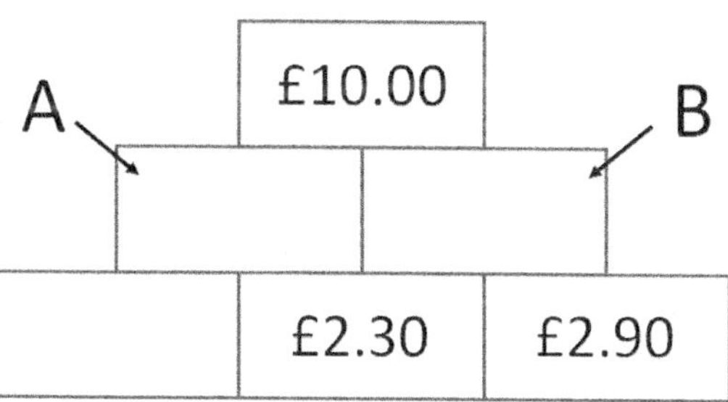

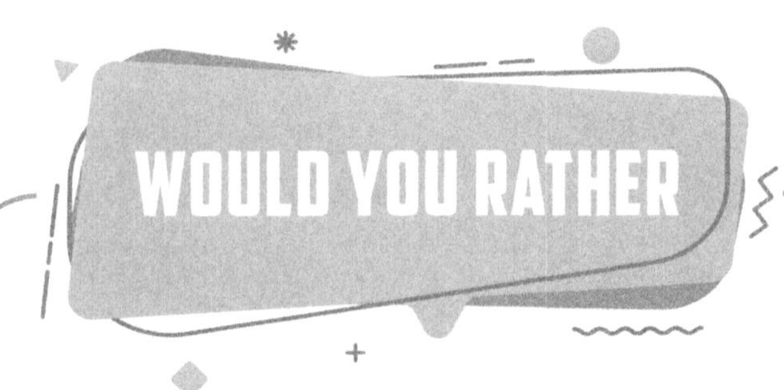

The **mean** of all the numbers here

OR

the **mode** of all the numbers

10   3   8

7   8   7   5

3   13   4

9   4   8   9

Have double the
number of vertices

OR

the number of edges
on these shapes?

TRIANGULAR
PYRAMID

SQUARE
PYRAMID

HEXAGONAL
PYRAMID

Have the value of the tenths plus the hundredths in the number below

OR

double the value of the thousandths?

0.35192

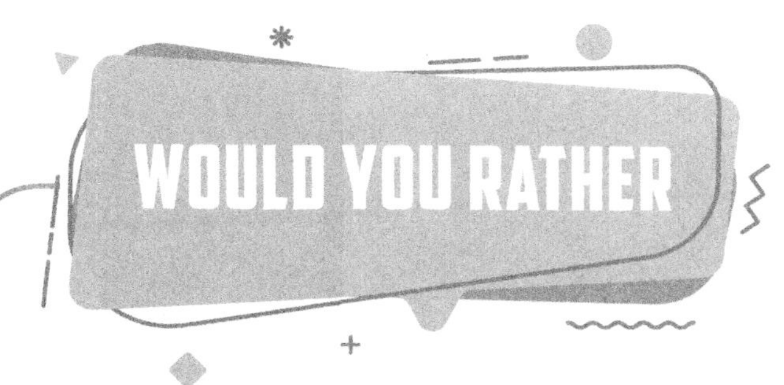

Have the sum of all
the even numbers

OR

the sum of all the
odd numbers?

476   257   109

358   125

513   725   922

Have the sum of
CLXI + LXVI + CXVII

OR

A third of MLXVI?

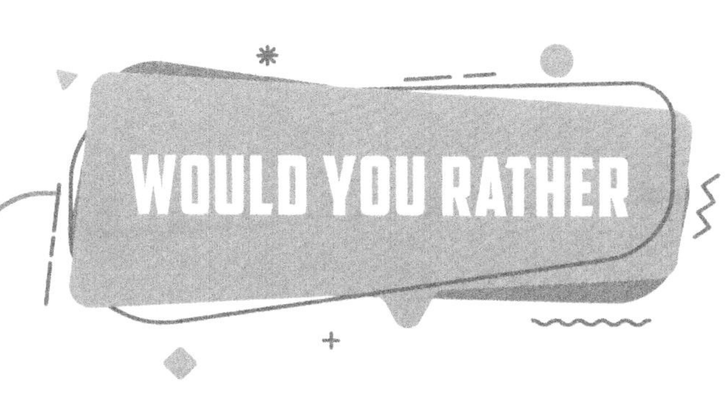

Multiply

OR

Divide?

You have 16 metres of ribbon to put in gift boxes. Each box should have the same amount of ribbon.

How much ribbon will each of the 20 boxes get?

Have the sum of the three largest numbers on the right

OR

the sum of the three smallest numbers
on the left?

<table>
<tr><td>8.1   12.5
17.45
15.1   7.3</td><td>0.9   4.95
13.6
4.02   8.8</td></tr>
</table>

Have the value of
F+I+R+E

OR

the value of
W+O+O+D

A	B	C	D	E	F	G	H	I	J	K	L	M
1	2	3	4	5	6	7	8	9	10	11	12	13

N	O	P	Q	R	S	T	U	V	W	X	Y	Z
14	15	16	17	18	19	20	21	22	23	24	25	26

Have $6^2 \times 3^2$

OR

$9^2 + 9^2$.

Have $4^2 \times 5^2$

OR

$2^2 + 3^2 + 4^2 + 5^2 + 6^2$?

Say, "Always!"

OR

say, "Never!"?

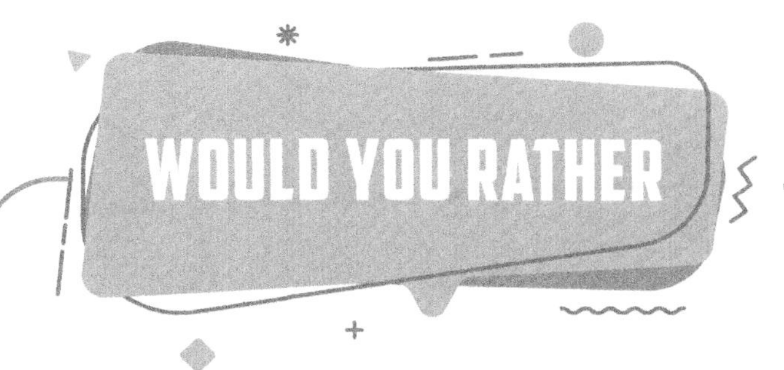

Have the number of hours
left until the end of the year

OR

the number of minutes
left until midnight?

It is 21:48 on December 25th

Have the product of the numbers at 24,25 and 27,22

OR

the product of the numbers at 25,26 and 23,24?

26	82	92	79	53	64	62
25	13	85	58	78	87	56
24	43	62	65	49	82	29
23	88	64	45	81	12	57
22	25	82	96	77	19	67
21	39	99	90	17	97	46
	23	24	25	26	27	28

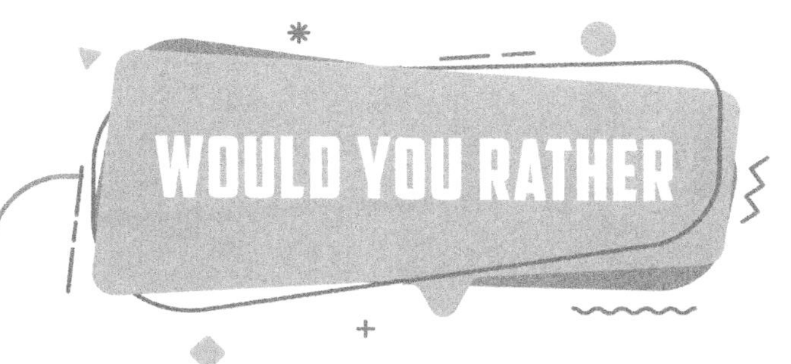

Have a third of the product of eighteen and twenty-five

OR

CM ÷ IX

Have the value of
your first and second initials
multiplied together

OR

the value of all the letters
in your second name
added together?

A	B	C	D	E	F	G	H	I	J	K	L	M
1	2	3	4	5	6	7	8	9	10	11	12	13

N	O	P	Q	R	S	T	U	V	W	X	Y	Z
14	15	16	17	18	19	20	21	22	23	24	25	26

Have

🥦 + 🥦 + 🥦

OR

🍉 + 🍉 + 🍉

🍉 + 🍉 + 🥦 = 72

🥦 + 🥦 + 🍉 = 66

Thank you for downloading and reading this book, you're a rockstar!

I hope you enjoyed making, and talking about all the mathematical choices. If you've found this book useful please leave a review. Even a few words would help others to decide if the book is right for them.

Thank you again - and remember...

"MATHS IS FOR EVERYONE AND EVERYTHING YOU DO COUNTS!"

John

mathsticks.com